Family Living

Our Favorite
CUPCAKES & MORE

Cupcakes, muffins, and rolls…oh, my!
Treats so tiny and tasty are impossible to resist.
These recipes offer yummy choices for all occasions.

Delicious little cakes for fun parties and snacking!
Cupcakes • Muffins • Biscuits • Pastries • Breads • Mini Cakes

D1735977

Little Rock, Arkansas

MINT BROWNIE BITES

- 4 ounces unsweetened chocolate
- 1 cup butter or margarine
- 3 eggs
- 1 cup granulated sugar
- 1 cup brown sugar, firmly packed
- 1 teaspoon vanilla extract
- 1/4 teaspoon almond extract
- 1 cup all-purpose flour
- 1/4 teaspoon salt
- 3/4 cup chopped walnuts
- 2/3 cup chopped Andes® chocolate mint wafer candies

In a small saucepan, melt chocolate and butter over low heat, stirring until smooth. Remove from heat and cool completely.

Preheat oven to 350 degrees. In a large bowl, beat eggs and sugar 3 minutes or until thick and creamy. Stir in extracts and chocolate mixture. Add flour and salt, stirring until mixture is completely blended. Stir in walnuts and chopped candies. Spoon batter into buttered miniature muffin pans, filling pans two-thirds full. Bake 15 to 20 minutes or until brownies begin to pull away from sides of pan. Cool completely before removing from pans. Store in airtight container.

Yield: about 4 dozen brownies

RED-WHITE-AND-BLUE MUFFINS

- 2 cups all-purpose flour
- 1 cup quick-cooking oats
- 1/3 cup firmly packed brown sugar
- 1/3 cup granulated sugar
- 3/4 teaspoon baking soda
- 3/4 teaspoon baking powder
- 1/4 teaspoon salt
- 3/4 cup buttermilk
- 1/2 cup butter or margarine, melted
- 2 eggs
- 1 teaspoon vanilla extract
- 1 package (12 ounces) vanilla baking chips
- 1 cup coarsely chopped maraschino cherries
- 1 cup fresh blueberries

Preheat oven to 375 degrees. In a large bowl, combine flour, oats, sugars, baking soda, baking powder, and salt. Form a well in center of dry ingredients. In a small bowl, combine buttermilk, melted butter, eggs, and vanilla. Add liquid to dry ingredients; stir just until moistened. Stir in vanilla chips, cherries, and blueberries. Fill paper-lined muffin cups two-thirds full. Bake 18 to 22 minutes or until lightly browned. Transfer muffins to a wire rack to cool. Store in an airtight container.

Yield: about 2 dozen muffins

Maraschino cherries, vanilla baking chips, and fresh blueberries are baked into these moist little Red-White-And-Blue Muffins for bite after bite of star-spangled flavor.

ROSE PETAL TEA CAKES

Shown on front cover.

Sugared Rose Petals must be made 1 day in advance.

SUGARED ROSE PETALS
   2 egg whites
      Rose petals from pesticide-free blossoms, washed and patted dry
      Granulated sugar

CAKES
   $1/2$ cup butter or margarine, softened
   4 ounces cream cheese, softened
   1 cup granulated sugar
   2 eggs
   $1/2$ cup sour cream
   2 tablespoons milk
   1 tablespoon rose flower water (available at gourmet food stores)
   $1 2/3$ cups all-purpose flour
   $1/2$ teaspoon baking soda
   $1/2$ teaspoon baking powder
   $1/2$ teaspoon ground nutmeg
   $1/4$ teaspoon salt
   1 cup chopped pecans
      Pink paste food coloring (optional)

FROSTING
   1 cup whipping cream
   1 package (8 ounces) cream cheese, softened
   $1/4$ cup granulated sugar
   1 tablespoon rose flower water
      Silk rose leaves to decorate

For sugared rose petals, place egg whites in a small bowl. Dip rose petals in egg whites. Hold dipped rose petals over a sheet of waxed paper and sprinkle generously with sugar. Transfer to waxed paper-covered rolling pin to retain shape of petals. Allow to dry at room temperature 24 hours or until hardened.

For cakes, preheat oven to 350 degrees. In a large bowl, cream butter, cream cheese, and sugar until fluffy. Add eggs, sour cream, milk, and rose flower water; stir until smooth. In a medium bowl, sift together flour, baking soda, baking powder, nutmeg, and salt. Add dry ingredients to creamed mixture, stirring until smooth. Stir in pecans. If desired, tint batter light pink. Pour into a greased and floured shortcake pan, filling each tin $2/3$ full. Bake 15 to 20 minutes, using a toothpick to test for doneness. Cool in pan 10 minutes. Remove from pan and cool completely on a wire rack.

For frosting, place a medium bowl and beaters from an electric mixer in freezer until well chilled. In chilled bowl, beat cream until soft peaks form; refrigerate. In a large bowl, beat cream cheese, sugar, and rose flower water until fluffy. Gradually add whipped cream to cream cheese mixture; beat until smooth and stiff peaks form. Frost tops of cakes. To decorate, arrange rose petals and silk leaves on tops of cakes. Cover and refrigerate until ready to present. Remove leaves before eating.
Yield: about 1 dozen tea cakes

IRISH CREAM CAKES

CAKES
- 1 package (18.25 ounces) white cake mix
- 1 1/2 cups Irish cream liqueur
- 1 cup miniature semisweet chocolate chips
- 4 eggs
- 1 package (6 ounces) instant vanilla pudding mix
- 1/2 cup vegetable oil

GLAZE
- 3 cups confectioners sugar
- 1 cup Irish cream liqueur

Preheat oven to 350 degrees. For cakes, combine cake mix, liqueur, chocolate chips, eggs, pudding mix, and oil in a large mixing bowl; blend well. Pour into 10 greased and floured 1-cup metal gelatin or cake molds. Bake 25 to 30 minutes or until cake springs back when lightly touched.

For glaze, combine confectioners sugar and liqueur in a small bowl; blend well. While cakes are still warm in molds, poke holes in cakes; pour glaze over. Allow cakes to cool in molds at least 2 hours before removing.

Yield: 10 miniature cakes

APRICOT BREAD

- 3/4 cup butter or margarine, softened
- 3/4 cup sugar
- 2 eggs, lightly beaten
- 1 cup chopped dried apricots
- 1/2 cup toasted coconut
- 1/4 cup orange juice
- 1 teaspoon grated orange zest
- 1 teaspoon ground cinnamon
- 3 cups all-purpose flour
- 1 teaspoon salt
- 1 teaspoon baking soda
- 1 cup sour cream
- 1/2 cup chopped walnuts

Preheat oven to 350 degrees. In a large bowl, cream butter and sugar until fluffy. Beat in eggs. Stir in apricots, coconut, orange juice, orange zest, and cinnamon. In a medium bowl, combine flour, salt, and baking soda. Alternately stir dry ingredients and sour cream into apricot mixture. Stir in walnuts. Pour batter into a greased 5 x 9 x 3-inch loaf pan. Bake 1 hour or until a toothpick inserted in center of bread comes out clean. Remove from pan and cool on wire rack. Store in an airtight container.

Yield: 1 loaf bread

STICKY BUNS

2 packages dry yeast
$^1/_3$ cup granulated sugar
1 teaspoon salt
$^1/_4$ cup milk
$^1/_2$ cup buttermilk
1 tablespoon orange juice
$^1/_2$ teaspoon grated orange zest
1 teaspoon vanilla extract
2 egg yolks
3 cups all-purpose flour, divided
1 cup butter or margarine, softened
4 teaspoons ground cinnamon
1 cup raisins
2 cups firmly packed brown sugar, divided
$^1/_2$ cup honey
1 cup chopped pecans
$^1/_4$ cup butter or margarine, melted

In a large bowl, combine yeast, granulated sugar, and salt. Beat in milk, buttermilk, orange juice, orange zest, and vanilla until smooth. Stir in egg yolks and $1^1/_2$ cups of flour. Stir in butter and remaining $1^1/_2$ cups flour.

On a lightly floured surface, knead dough until smooth and elastic (about 10 minutes). Place dough in a lightly greased bowl. Cover and chill at least 2 hours or until well chilled.

Preheat oven to 350 degrees. On a lightly floured surface, knead dough again until smooth. Using a floured rolling pin, roll out dough into a $^1/_4$-inch-thick rectangle about 10 x 18 inches. Sprinkle with cinnamon, raisins, and 1 cup brown sugar. Beginning at 1 long edge, roll up dough jellyroll style. Cut into $^3/_4$-inch-thick slices.

In a small bowl, combine remaining 1 cup brown sugar, honey, and pecans. Grease four 6-cup jumbo muffin tins. Place 1 tablespoon pecan mixture in each muffin cup. Place a slice of dough on top of pecan mixture. Brush tops of dough with melted butter. Bake 35 to 40 minutes or until golden brown. Turn sticky buns onto waxed paper to cool completely. Store in an airtight container.
Yield: 2 dozen buns

Sticky Buns are sweet yeast rolls filled with cinnamon and raisins and topped with a honey glaze of brown sugar and pecans.

Crowned with a fluffy swirl of red, white, and blue icing, Stars and Stripes Muffins have all-American appeal. Easily prepared with blueberry muffin mix, each patriotic pastry hides a cherry surprise inside.

STARS AND STRIPES MUFFINS

MUFFINS

  1 package (14 ounces) blueberry muffin mix, and ingredients required to prepare muffins
  ¹/₂ cup cherry preserves

ICING

  3 cups sifted confectioners sugar
  ¹/₃ cup vegetable shortening
  1¹/₂ teaspoons clear vanilla extract
  2 tablespoons milk
    Red and blue paste food coloring
    Small flags to decorate

Preheat oven to 400 degrees. For muffins, mix according to package directions. Place 1 tablespoon batter in foil muffin cups or in each cup of a greased and floured muffin tin. Spoon 1 teaspoon cherry preserves into center of batter. Top with 1 tablespoon muffin batter. Bake 16 to 19 minutes or until tops are light brown. Transfer to a wire rack to cool completely.

For icing, combine first 4 ingredients in a large bowl; beat until smooth. Use a small paintbrush to paint a stripe of red and a stripe of blue food coloring inside a pastry bag fitted with a large star tip. Spoon icing into pastry bag. Pipe icing onto muffins. Decorate with flags. Store in an airtight container.

Yield: 12 muffins

7

CHERRY MUFFINS

1 jar (10 ounces) maraschino cherries
1³/₄ cups all-purpose flour
¹/₂ cup granulated sugar
2¹/₂ teaspoons baking powder
1 teaspoon dried grated lemon peel
³/₄ teaspoon salt
1 egg
¹/₂ cup milk
¹/₃ cup vegetable oil
1 teaspoon almond extract
¹/₄ cup chopped almonds

Preheat oven to 400 degrees. Reserving ¹/₄ cup cherry juice, drain and coarsely chop cherries.

In a large bowl, stir together flour, sugar, baking powder, lemon peel, and salt. Make a well in center of dry ingredients. In a small bowl, whisk reserved cherry juice, egg, milk, oil, and almond extract. Pour egg mixture into well in dry ingredients. Stir just until moistened. Stir in cherries and almonds. Spoon batter into a paper-lined muffin pan, filling each tin ³/₄ full. Bake 18 to 20 minutes or until edges are light brown. Transfer to a wire rack to cool completely. Store in an airtight container.
Yield: about 1 dozen muffins

JAMMIE MUFFINS

MUFFINS
1¹/₂ cups all-purpose flour
¹/₃ cup granulated sugar
2 teaspoons baking powder
¹/₂ teaspoon salt
1 egg, beaten
¹/₂ cup milk
¹/₄ cup vegetable oil
1 teaspoon vanilla extract
¹/₂ cup desired flavor jam, room temperature

TOPPING
2 tablespoons butter or margarine, melted
¹/₄ cup granulated sugar

Preheat oven to 400 degrees. In a large bowl, combine flour, sugar, baking powder, and salt. In a separate bowl, combine egg, milk, oil, and vanilla. Add to dry ingredients, stirring just until blended. Fill greased miniature muffin pans two-thirds full with batter. Top each with ¹/₄ teaspoon jam. Gently swirl jam into batter with a toothpick. Bake 12 to 15 minutes, testing for doneness with a toothpick. Remove from pans and brush tops with melted butter; sprinkle with sugar. Serve warm.
Yield: about 2 dozen muffins
To reheat: Wrap muffins in aluminum foil and bake in a 350 degree oven 10 minutes.

Sweet maraschino cherries and chopped almonds give these muffins their distinctive flavor.

9

CHERRY-NUT CAKES

12 ounces dried cherries (available at gourmet food stores)
1 1/2 cups orange-flavored liqueur
6 tablespoons finely chopped crystallized ginger
1 cup butter or margarine, softened
3/4 cup firmly packed brown sugar
6 eggs
1 tablespoon vanilla extract
1 1/2 cups all-purpose flour
1 teaspoon ground cinnamon
1/2 teaspoon ground nutmeg
1/4 teaspoon ground cloves
2 cups chopped unsalted pecans
2 cups chopped unsalted walnuts
2 cups chopped unsalted cashews

In a small bowl, combine cherries, liqueur, and ginger. Cover and let stand at room temperature 8 hours or overnight.

Preheat oven to 350 degrees. In a large bowl, cream butter and brown sugar until fluffy. Beat in eggs and vanilla. In a small bowl, combine flour, cinnamon, nutmeg, and cloves. Add flour mixture to creamed mixture; stir until smooth. Stir in cherry mixture and nuts. Spoon batter into greased and floured 2 1/2 x 4 1/2-inch loaf pans. Bake 35 to 40 minutes or until a toothpick inserted in center of cake comes out clean. Cool in pans 10 minutes; remove from pans and cool completely on a wire rack. Store in an airtight container.
Yield: about 1 1/2 dozen cakes

Shown on back cover: These Ice-Cream Cone Cupcakes are as much fun to make as they are to eat! Simply fill ice-cream cones with chocolate cake batter, bake, and decorate with icing and candies. Delivered in cellophane-wrapped plastic cups, your creations will stay fresh until party time.

ICE-CREAM CONE CUPCAKES

CUPCAKES
1 package (18.25 ounces) chocolate cake mix
1 1/4 cups water
1/2 cup vegetable oil
3 eggs
30 small flat-bottomed ice-cream cones

ICING
5 cups sifted confectioners sugar
3/4 cup vegetable shortening
1/2 cup butter or margarine, softened
2 1/2 tablespoons milk
1 1/4 teaspoons almond extract
Assorted purchased sprinkles and candies to decorate

For cupcakes, preheat oven to 350 degrees. In a large bowl, combine first 4 ingredients according to cake mix package directions. Fill each cone with about 2 1/2 tablespoons of batter. Place cones about 3 inches apart on an ungreased baking sheet. Bake 25 to 30 minutes or untiil a toothpick inserted in center of cupcake comes out clean. Cool completely.

For icing, beat all ingredients together in a large bowl until smooth. Ice each cupcake with about 1 tablespoon icing. Before icing hardens, decorate with sprinkles and candies. Store in an airtight container.
Yield: 30 cupcakes

FUZZY NAVEL CAKES

- 1 package (18.25 ounces) yellow cake mix
- 4 eggs
- $3/4$ cup peach schnapps
- 1 package (6 ounces) instant vanilla pudding mix
- $1/2$ cup vegetable oil
- $1/2$ cup orange juice
- $1/2$ teaspoon orange extract
- 1 cup peach schnapps
- 2 tablespoons orange juice
- 3 cups confectioners sugar, sifted

Preheat oven to 350 degrees. Combine first 7 ingredients in mixing bowl and blend well. Pour into 10 greased and lightly floured 1-cup metal gelatin molds, filling half full. Bake 25 to 30 minutes or until cake springs back when lightly touched. Combine 1 cup peach schnapps, 2 tablespoons orange juice, and confectioners sugar. While cakes are still warm in molds, poke holes in cakes; pour liqueur mixture over. Allow cakes to cool in molds at least 2 hours before removing.
Yield: 10 small cakes

CHOCOLATE-KAHLÚA CAKE

- 1 package (18.25 ounces) chocolate cake mix
- 4 eggs
- $3/4$ cup Kahlúa liqueur
- 1 package (6 ounces) instant chocolate pudding mix
- $1/2$ cup vegetable oil
- $1/2$ cup water
- 6 tablespoons Kahlúa liqueur
- 1 cup confectioners sugar, sifted

Preheat oven to 350 degrees. Combine first 6 ingredients in mixing bowl and blend well. Pour into greased and lightly floured 10-inch fluted tube pan. Bake 45 to 50 minutes or until cake springs back when lightly touched. Combine 6 tablespoons Kahlúa and confectioners sugar. While cake is still warm in pan, poke holes in cake; pour liqueur mixture over. Allow cake to cool in pan at least 2 hours before removing.
Yield: 1 cake

GOLDEN AMARETTO CAKES

- 1 package (18.25 ounces) yellow cake mix
- 4 eggs
- $3/4$ cup amaretto
- 1 package (6 ounces) instant vanilla pudding mix
- $1/2$ cup vegetable oil
- $1/2$ cup water
- $1/4$ teaspoon almond extract
- 6 tablespoons amaretto
- 1 cup confectioners sugar, sifted

Preheat oven to 350 degrees. Combine first 7 ingredients in mixing bowl and blend well. Pour into 2 greased and lightly floured 6-cup metal gelatin molds. Bake 40 to 45 minutes or until cake springs back when lightly touched. Combine 6 tablespoons amaretto and confectioners sugar. While cakes are still warm in molds, poke holes in cakes; pour liqueur mixture over. Allow cakes to cool in molds at least 2 hours before removing.
Yield: 2 cakes

CHERRY-ALMOND BREAD

1 cup granulated sugar
$1/2$ cup butter or margarine, softened
2 eggs
2 cups all-purpose flour
1 teaspoon baking soda
$1/2$ teaspoon salt
1 cup buttermilk
1 cup chopped almonds
1 jar (10 ounces) maraschino
   cherries, drained and chopped
1 teaspoon almond extract

Preheat oven to 350 degrees. In a large bowl, cream sugar, butter, and eggs until light and fluffy. In a separate bowl, sift together flour, baking soda, and salt. Blend into creamed mixture with buttermilk. Stir in almonds, cherries, and almond extract. Pour batter into a greased and floured 9 x 5 x 3-inch loaf pan and bake 55 to 60 minutes, testing for doneness with a toothpick. Remove from pan and cool on a wire rack.
Yield: 1 loaf of bread

BLUEBERRY-LEMON BREAD

3 tablespoons shortening
3 tablespoons butter or margarine
1 cup granulated sugar
1 tablespoon grated lemon peel
2 eggs
1 tablespoon fresh lemon juice
$1^1/2$ cups all-purpose flour
1 teaspoon baking powder
$1/4$ teaspoon salt
$1/2$ cup milk
1 cup fresh or frozen blueberries (if frozen, do not thaw)
2 tablespoons all-purpose flour

Preheat oven to 350 degrees. In a large bowl, cream shortening, butter, sugar, and lemon peel. Add eggs and lemon juice, mixing well. In a separate bowl, sift together $1^1/2$ cups flour, baking powder, and salt. Blend into creamed mixture with milk. Toss blueberries with 2 tablespoons flour. Gently fold into batter. Pour batter into a greased and floured 9 x 5 x 3-inch loaf pan and bake 50 to 55 minutes, testing for doneness with a toothpick. Remove from pan and cool on a wire rack.
Yield: 1 loaf of bread

Whether the baby's a boy or a girl, you'll be ready to congratulate the new mother with one of these sweet quick breads. Tangy Blueberry-Lemon Bread is easy to coordinate with gifts for a boy, and delicate Cherry-Almond Bread looks pretty for a girl.

POPPY SEED CAKE

CAKE
- $1/2$ cup poppy seed
- $1/3$ cup milk
- 1 cup butter or margarine, softened
- $1^1/2$ cups granulated sugar
- 2 teaspoons grated lemon peel
- $1^1/2$ teaspoons lemon extract
- 1 teaspoon vanilla extract
- 4 eggs
- $2^1/4$ cups all-purpose flour
- $1^1/2$ teaspoons baking powder
- $1/2$ teaspoon salt
- $1/2$ cup sour cream

GLAZE
- $1/2$ cup confectioners sugar
- $1/4$ cup lemon juice

Soak poppy seed in milk 1 hour.

Preheat oven to 350 degrees. For cake, cream butter, sugar, lemon peel, and extracts in a large mixing bowl. Beat in eggs, one at a time, beating well after each addition. Drain poppy seed; stir poppy seed into mixture. In a medium bowl, combine flour, baking powder, and salt. Stir flour mixture into creamed mixture, alternating with sour cream. Pour into a greased and floured $9^1/4$ x $5^1/4$ x $2^1/2$-inch loaf pan. Bake 45 to 50 minutes or until a toothpick inserted in center of cake comes out clean.

For glaze, combine confectioners sugar and lemon juice, blending until smooth. Pour over warm cake in pan. Allow cake to cool completely before removing from pan.

Yield: 10 to 12 servings

POPPY SEED ROSETTES

- 1 tablespoon sugar
- 1 package dry yeast
- $1^1/2$ cups warm water
- $3^1/2$ to 4 cups all-purpose flour, divided
- $1^1/2$ teaspoons salt
  Vegetable cooking spray
- 1 egg white
- 1 tablespoon water
  Poppy seed

In a small bowl, dissolve sugar and yeast in $1^1/2$ cups warm water. In a large bowl, combine 2 cups flour and salt. Add yeast mixture to dry ingredients; beat with an electric mixer until well blended. Add $1^1/4$ cups flour; stir until a soft dough forms. Turn onto a lightly floured surface. Knead about 5 minutes or until dough becomes smooth and elastic, using additional flour as necessary. Place in a large bowl sprayed with cooking spray, turning once to coat top of dough. Cover and let rise in a warm place (80 to 85 degrees) about $1^1/2$ hours or until doubled in size.

Turn dough onto a lightly floured surface and punch down. Cover and allow dough to rest 10 minutes. Divide dough into 20 equal pieces. Roll each piece of dough into a 12-inch rope. Loosely tie each rope into a knot, tucking ends either into or under dough to form rosette. Place on a lightly greased baking sheet. Spray tops of rolls with cooking spray, cover, and let rise in a warm place about $1^1/2$ hours or until nearly doubled in size.

Preheat oven to 375 degrees. In a small bowl, lightly beat egg white and water. Brush rolls with egg mixture. Bake 8 minutes. Remove from oven and brush with egg white mixture again; sprinkle with poppy seeds. Bake 16 to 18 minutes or until golden brown. Serve warm or transfer to a wire rack to cool completely.

Yield: 20 rolls.

CHOCOLATE MERINGUE CUPCAKES

CRUST
- 16 2-inch-diameter chocolate wafer cookies, finely ground
- 3 tablespoons butter or margarine, melted
- 1 teaspoon ground cinnamon

FILLING
- 3 egg whites
- $2/3$ cup sugar
- $1/2$ teaspoon ground cinnamon
- $1/2$ cup semisweet chocolate chips
- $1/2$ cup chopped pecans

For crust, combine cookie crumbs, butter, and cinnamon in a medium bowl; stir until well blended. Line a muffin pan with foil muffin cups. Press about 2 teaspoons mixture into bottom of each muffin cup.

Preheat oven to 325 degrees. For filling, beat egg whites in a large bowl until foamy. Gradually adding sugar and cinnamon, beat until stiff. Fold in chocolate chips and pecans. Spoon about 2 tablespoons filling into each muffin cup. Bake 30 to 35 minutes or until lightly browned and set in center. Cool completely in pan. Store in an airtight container.

Yield: about $1^1/2$ dozen cupcakes

MINIATURE TOFFEE CHEESECAKES

CRUST
- $1/2$ cup butter or margarine, softened
- $1/2$ cup firmly packed brown sugar
- 1 teaspoon vanilla extract
- $1^1/4$ cups all-purpose flour
- $1/2$ cup finely chopped pecans

FILLING
- 2 packages (8 ounces each) cream cheese, softened
- $1/2$ cup firmly packed brown sugar
- 2 eggs
- 1 teaspoon vanilla-butter-nut flavoring
- 1 package (6 ounces) milk chocolate-covered toffee bits

For crust, cream butter, brown sugar, and vanilla in a medium bowl until fluffy. Add flour; stir until well blended. Stir in pecans. Press 1 teaspoon crust mixture into bottom of each paper-lined cup of a miniature muffin pan.

Preheat oven to 350 degrees. For filling, beat cream cheese and brown sugar in a medium bowl until fluffy. Add eggs and vanilla-butter-nut flavoring; beat until well blended. Stir in toffee bits. Spoon 1 tablespoon filling mixture over each crust. Bake 16 to 18 minutes or until filling is set in center. Place pan on a wire rack to cool. Store in refrigerator in an airtight container.

Yield: about 5 dozen miniature cheesecakes

DANISH PASTRIES

CAKE
- 1 1/2 cups butter, softened and divided
- 3 cups all-purpose flour, divided
- 1/8 teaspoon salt
- 1/4 cup cold water
- 1 cup milk
- 1/4 cup granulated sugar
- 1 teaspoon almond extract
- 3 eggs

GLAZE
- 1 1/2 cups confectioners sugar
- 2 tablespoons butter, softened
- 1 tablespoon milk
- 2 teaspoons vanilla extract

TOPPING
- 1 cup sliced almonds, toasted
- 2 tablespoons confectioners sugar

For cake, use a pastry blender or two knives to cut 1 cup butter into 2 cups flour in a medium mixing bowl until mixture resembles coarse meal. Stir in salt and water to make a dough. Divide dough into eight equal portions. Pat out each portion of dough into a 3 x 4-inch oval on an ungreased baking sheet. Refrigerate until ready to use.

Preheat oven to 350 degrees. In a large heavy saucepan, combine remaining 1/2 cup butter and milk over medium heat. Bring to a boil. Add remaining 1 cup flour, sugar, and almond extract. Quickly stir until mixture forms a ball; remove from heat. By hand, beat in eggs, one at a time, until well blended. Spread a thick, even layer of dough over chilled ovals. Bake 40 to 45 minutes or until puffy and golden.

For glaze, combine confectioners sugar and butter in a small bowl; stir until well blended. Stir in milk and vanilla until mixture is smooth.

For topping, mix almonds with confectioners sugar in a small bowl.

Spread glaze evenly over warm pastries. Sprinkle each pastry with topping. Serve warm or at room temperature.
Yield: 8 pastries

SANTA DANISH ROLLS

ROLLS
- 1 package (11 ounces) refrigerated orange Danish rolls
- 1/4 cup all-purpose flour
- 1 egg white
- 1 tablespoon cold water
- Red paste food coloring

ICING
- 1 1/3 cups confectioners sugar
- 1 egg white
- 1/8 teaspoon cream of tartar
- Licorice, red cinnamon candies, and miniature marshmallows to decorate

Preheat oven to 375 degrees. Unroll each piece of dough and gently brush away cinnamon filling. Sprinkle flour over work area. With lightly floured hands, shape each piece of dough into a ball. Roll lightly in flour. Shape into a smooth oval and place on a greased baking sheet. Pinch top of oval to form a Santa hat. In small cup, combine egg white, water, and food coloring.

(Continued on page 17.)

Prepared with refrigerated breakfast rolls, Santa Danish Rolls make a sweet Christmas morning surprise.

(Continued from page 16.)
Referring to photo, paint hat and cheeks on each roll. Bake 11 to 15 minutes or until lightly browned. Remove from oven. While rolls are still hot, touch up hats and cheeks with colored egg white. Place on wire racks to cool.

For icing, combine sugar, egg white, and cream of tartar in a small bowl and beat until stiff, about 5 minutes.

Immediately spoon icing into a pastry bag fitted with a small star tip. For beard and hat trim, refer to photo and pipe icing onto each roll. For face and hat, attach candy pieces and a marshmallow to each roll with icing. Store in airtight container.
Yield: 8 Santa rolls

ORANGE-OATMEAL ROLLS

1 package (16 ounces) hot roll mix
1 cup sweetened crunchy oat cereal
1 cup very warm orange juice (120 to 130 degrees)
2 tablespoons honey
2 tablespoons butter or margarine, melted
1 egg
1 tablespoon grated orange zest
1/2 cup coarsely ground pecans
  Vegetable cooking spray
1 cup sifted confectioners sugar
5 teaspoons orange juice

In a large bowl, combine hot roll mix and yeast from roll mix with cereal. Stir in 1 cup very warm orange juice, honey, melted butter, egg, and orange zest; stir until well blended. Stir in pecans. Turn onto a lightly floured surface and knead 3 minutes or until dough becomes smooth and elastic. Cover dough; allow to rest 10 minutes. Shape dough into eighteen 2-inch balls. Place in 2 greased 8 x 5-inch aluminum foil baking pans. Spray tops of dough with cooking spray, cover, and let rise in a warm place (80 to 85 degrees) 1 hour or until almost doubled in size.

Preheat oven to 375 degrees. Bake 15 to 20 minutes or until golden brown. Cool in pans. Combine confectioners sugar and 5 teaspoons orange juice in a small bowl; stir until smooth. Drizzle icing over rolls. Allow icing to harden. Store in an airtight container.

Yield: 2 pans rolls, 9 rolls each

RAISIN-WALNUT PINWHEELS

1 sheet (from a 17 1/4-ounce package) frozen puff pastry dough, thawed
1/3 cup granulated sugar
1 tablespoon ground cinnamon
1/4 cup butter or margarine
1/2 cup raisins
1/2 cup finely chopped walnuts
1 egg yolk, beaten

Preheat oven to 350 degrees. On a lightly floured surface, use a floured rolling pin to roll out pastry to an 8 x 12-inch rectangle. In a small bowl, combine sugar and cinnamon and set aside. In a small saucepan, melt butter. Add raisins and walnuts, stirring until well coated. Spread raisin mixture evenly over pastry. Sprinkle sugar mixture evenly over raisin mixture. Beginning at 1 long edge, roll up pastry. Brush egg yolk on long edge to seal. Place on a greased baking sheet. Bake 20 to 25 minutes or until golden brown. Cool completely. Cut into 1-inch slices.

Yield: about 12 pinwheels

NUTTY SWEET POTATO MUFFINS

TOPPING
- 1/2 cup firmly packed brown sugar
- 1/2 cup all-purpose flour
- 1/2 cup chopped pecans
- 3 tablespoons vegetable oil
- 1/2 teaspoon ground cinnamon

MUFFINS
- 2 1/4 cups all-purpose flour
- 1 1/2 teaspoons ground cinnamon
- 1 teaspoon baking soda
- 1/2 teaspoon ground allspice
- 1/2 teaspoon salt
- 1 cup previously cooked mashed sweet potatoes (or canned sweet potatoes, drained and mashed)
- 1 cup sugar
- 1/2 cup vegetable oil
- 2 eggs
- 1/2 teaspoon vanilla extract
- 1/2 cup chopped pecans

Preheat oven to 350 degrees. For topping, combine brown sugar, flour, pecans, oil, and cinnamon in a small bowl until well blended.

For muffins, combine flour, cinnamon, baking soda, allspice, and salt in a medium bowl. In another medium bowl, beat sweet potatoes, sugar, oil, eggs, and vanilla. Add dry ingredients to sweet potato mixture; beat until well blended. Stir in pecans. Fill greased muffin cups two-thirds full. Sprinkle about 1 1/2 tablespoons topping over batter in each cup. Bake 20 to 25 minutes or until a toothpick inserted in center of muffin comes out clean. Cool in pan 5 minutes. Serve warm or transfer muffins to a wire rack to cool completely.
Yield: about 16 muffins

BLACKBERRY CUPCAKES

- 1 cup butter or margarine, softened
- 3/4 cup granulated sugar
- 2 eggs
- 1 cup blackberry jam
- 3/4 teaspoon vanilla extract
- 1 3/4 cups all-purpose flour
- 1/8 teaspoon salt
- 1/2 cup whipping cream
- 1 cup chopped pecans
- Confectioners sugar

Preheat oven to 350 degrees. In a large bowl, cream butter and granulated sugar until fluffy. Add eggs 1 at a time, beating well after each addition. Beat in jam and vanilla. In a medium bowl, sift together flour and salt. Add dry ingredients alternately with whipping cream to creamed mixture; stir until well blended. Fold in pecans. Spoon batter into paper-lined muffin tins, filling each tin 2/3 full. Bake 30 to 35 minutes or until a toothpick inserted in center comes out clean. Transfer to a wire rack to cool completely. Dust with confectioners sugar. Store in an airtight container.
Yield: about 2 dozen cupcakes

Kids will be "hoppy" to help make—and eat—Easter Basket Cupcakes.

EASTER BASKET CUPCAKES

1¹/₃ cups flaked coconut
Green liquid food coloring
1 package (18.25 ounces) chocolate fudge cake mix with pudding in the mix
1¹/₃ cups water
3 eggs
¹/₃ cup vegetable oil
2 containers (16 ounces each) vanilla ready-to-spread frosting
Vanilla wafers, graham cereal squares, small jellybeans, and red string licorice to decorate

Preheat oven to 350 degrees. Place coconut in a small bowl; tint light green. In a medium bowl, combine cake mix, water, eggs, and oil. Beat at low speed of an electric mixer 30 seconds. Beat at medium speed 2 minutes. Fill greased and floured muffin cups about two-thirds full. Bake 18 to 23 minutes or until a toothpick inserted in center of cupcake comes out clean. Cool in pan 5 minutes. Remove from pan and cool completely on a wire rack.

If necessary, use a serrated knife to level tops of cupcakes. Frost sides and tops of cupcakes. Press vanilla wafers or cereal pieces onto sides of cupcakes. Sprinkle tinted coconut on tops of cupcakes. Press jellybeans into centers of cupcakes for eggs. Twist 2 pieces of licorice together to make each handle. Press a handle into each cupcake.
Yield: about 2 dozen cupcakes

Beautifully decorated with tinted icing, Easter Egg Cakes have a hidden surprise inside—a yummy "yolk" made of sweetened cream cheese. The recipe is on page 22.

EASTER EGG CAKES

Shown on page 21.

CAKES
1 box (18.25 ounces) white cake mix without pudding mix
1¹/₄ cups water
¹/₃ cup vegetable oil
3 egg whites (reserve 1 egg yolk for filling)

FILLING
4 ounces cream cheese, softened
¹/₄ cup granulated sugar
1 egg yolk (reserved from cakes)
Yellow paste food coloring

ICING
6¹/₄ cups plus 2 tablespoons sifted confectioners sugar
¹/₂ cup water
2 tablespoons light corn syrup
1 teaspoon almond extract
Pink paste food coloring

ROYAL ICING
4 cups sifted confectioners sugar
3 egg whites
Pink, yellow, blue, and green paste food coloring

For cakes, preheat oven to 350 degrees. In a large bowl, combine cake mix, water, oil, and egg whites; beat until moistened using low speed of an electric mixer. Beat at medium speed 2 minutes.

For filling, beat cream cheese, sugar, and egg yolk in a medium bowl until smooth. Tint filling yellow. Spoon about 1 tablespoon cake batter into each tin of a greased and floured miniature egg pan containing six 3¹/₂-inch-long tins. Spoon about 1 teaspoon filling in center of batter. Continue filling each tin with batter until ³/₄ full. Bake 18 to 20 minutes or until cakes pull away from sides of pan and spring back when lightly pressed. Cool in pan 10 minutes. Invert onto a wire rack with waxed paper underneath to cool completely.

For icing, place sugar in a medium saucepan. In a small bowl, combine water and corn syrup. Add corn syrup mixture to sugar and stir until well blended. Attach candy thermometer to pan, making sure thermometer does not touch bottom of pan. Stirring constantly, cook over medium-low heat until icing reaches 100 degrees. Remove from heat; stir in almond extract. Tint icing light pink. Cool icing 5 minutes. Stirring icing occasionally, ice tops of cakes. Allow icing to harden.

For royal icing, beat sugar and egg whites in a medium bowl 7 to 10 minutes or until stiff. Divide icing evenly into 4 bowls. Tint icing pink, yellow, blue, and green. Transfer icings to separate pastry bags and use desired tips to decorate cakes. Allow icing to harden. Store in an airtight container.
Yield: about 2 dozen cakes

CINNAMON-BANANA BREAD

BREAD
1 cup firmly packed brown sugar
1 cup butter or margarine, divided
2 ripe bananas, cut into small pieces
$^1/_2$ cup chopped pecans
$^1/_2$ cup granulated sugar
2 eggs
$1^3/_4$ cups all-purpose flour
2 tablespoons ground cinnamon
1 teaspoon baking powder
$^1/_2$ teaspoon baking soda

FROSTING
$1^1/_4$ cups confectioners sugar
1 package (3 ounces) cream cheese, softened

Preheat oven to 350 degrees. For bread, combine brown sugar and $^1/_2$ cup butter in a medium saucepan over medium heat, stirring until butter is melted. Add bananas and pecans, stirring until well coated. Cool to room temperature.

In a large bowl, cream remaining butter and granulated sugar until fluffy. Beat in eggs. In a small bowl, sift together remaining ingredients. Stir dry ingredients into creamed mixture. Stir in banana mixture. Divide batter evenly between 2 greased $3^1/_2$ x $6^3/_4$-inch loaf pans. Bake 45 to 50 minutes or until a toothpick inserted in center of bread comes out clean. Cool in pans 10 minutes. Transfer to a wire rack to cool completely.

For frosting, combine confectioners sugar and cream cheese in a medium bowl. Using medium speed of an electric mixer, beat until smooth. Drizzle frosting over bread. Store in an airtight container.
Yield: 2 loaves of bread

APPLE-CINNAMON-NUT BREAD

$1^1/_2$ cups all-purpose flour
1 cup sugar, divided
$^1/_2$ cup chopped pecans
$1^1/_2$ teaspoons baking powder
$^1/_2$ teaspoon salt
$^1/_2$ teaspoon ground cinnamon
$^1/_3$ cup vegetable oil
1 egg
$^1/_4$ cup orange juice
1 teaspoon vanilla extract
1 medium Granny Smith apple, peeled, cored, and thinly sliced

Preheat oven to 350 degrees. In a medium bowl, combine flour, $^3/_4$ cup sugar, pecans, baking powder, and salt. Combine remaining $^1/_4$ cup sugar and cinnamon in a small bowl; set aside. In another small bowl, whisk oil, egg, orange juice, and vanilla. Add oil mixture to dry ingredients; stir just until moistened. Spread half of batter into 4 greased and floured $2^1/_2$ x 5-inch loaf pans. Place a single layer of apple slices over batter. Sprinkle cinnamon-sugar mixture over apples. Spread remaining batter over apples. Bake 30 to 35 minutes or until a toothpick inserted in center of bread comes out clean and tops are lightly browned. Cool bread in pans on a wire rack 10 minutes. Transfer bread to wire rack to cool completely. Store in an airtight container.
Yield: 4 mini bread loaves

QUICKIE CINNAMON ROLLS

3/4 cup firmly packed brown sugar
1/4 cup butter or margarine
1 teaspoon ground cinnamon
1/4 cup chopped pecans
1 can (10 biscuits) refrigerated
   Texas-style biscuits

In a small saucepan over medium heat, stir brown sugar, butter, and cinnamon until butter melts. Pour butter mixture into a 9-inch round cake pan. Sprinkle pecans over butter mixture. Dip one side of each biscuit in mixture; place coated side up in pan. Cover and refrigerate (best if baked and eaten within 1 to 2 days).

Yield: 10 cinnamon rolls

To serve: Bake uncovered in a preheated 400-degree oven 12 to 18 minutes or until bread is light brown. Serve immediately.

CHOCOLATE–CINNAMON ROLLS

DOUGH
1 package quick-acting dry yeast
1 cup warm water
2 3/4 cups all-purpose flour
1/2 cup cocoa
1/2 cup sugar
1 teaspoon salt
1/4 cup egg substitute
1 1/2 tablespoons vegetable oil
   Vegetable cooking spray

FILLING
3 tablespoons sugar, divided
4 teaspoons ground cinnamon, divided
3 tablespoons reduced-calorie margarine, divided

1 1/3 cups reduced-fat chocolate chips, divided
Vegetable cooking spray

GLAZE
1/2 cup confectioners sugar
2 teaspoons water

For dough, dissolve yeast in 1 cup warm water in a small bowl. In a large bowl, combine flour, cocoa, sugar, and salt. Add egg substitute, oil, and yeast mixture to dry ingredients; stir until a soft dough forms. Turn onto a lightly floured surface and knead about 3 minutes or until dough becomes smooth and elastic. Place in a large bowl sprayed with cooking spray, turning once to coat top of dough. Cover and let rise in a warm place (80 to 85 degrees) 1 hour or until almost doubled in size.

For filling, combine 1 1/2 tablespoons sugar and 2 teaspoons cinnamon in a small bowl; set aside. Turn dough onto a lightly floured surface and punch down. Divide dough in half. Roll out half of dough to a 10 x 16-inch rectangle. Spread 1 1/2 tablespoons margarine over dough; sprinkle sugar mixture and 2/3 cup chocolate chips over dough. Beginning at 1 long edge, roll up tightly. Cut into 1-inch-wide slices and place, cut side down, in a lightly sprayed 8-inch square baking dish. Repeat with remaining ingredients. Lightly spray tops of dough with cooking spray, cover, and let rise in a warm place 1 hour or until almost doubled in size.

Preheat oven to 375 degrees. Bake 18 to 23 minutes.

For glaze, combine confectioners sugar and water in a small bowl; stir until smooth. Drizzle over warm rolls; serve warm.

Yield: 32 cinnamon rolls

Made with half the fat of traditional cinnamon rolls, Chocolate-Cinnamon Rolls are delicious served warm from the oven.

ORANGE-CHOCOLATE CHIP SCONES

2 cups all-purpose flour
1/4 cup sugar
2 teaspoons baking powder
1 teaspoon salt
1/2 cup butter or margarine, cut into pieces
2 eggs, lightly beaten
3 tablespoons orange juice
1 teaspoon vanilla extract
1 teaspoon grated orange zest
1/2 cup semisweet chocolate chips
1/2 cup coarsely chopped pecans, toasted
1 egg yolk
1 teaspoon water
1 tablespoon sugar

Preheat oven to 350 degrees. Lightly grease a 9-inch circle in center of a baking sheet.

In a medium bowl, combine flour, 1/4 cup sugar, baking powder, and salt. Using a pastry blender or 2 knives, cut butter into flour mixture until mixture resembles coarse meal. Make a well in the center of dry ingredients and add eggs, orange juice, vanilla, and orange zest. Stir just until dry ingredients are moistened. Stir in chocolate chips and pecans.

Pat dough into a 9-inch circle in center of baking sheet. In a small bowl, combine egg yolk and water and brush over dough. Sprinkle with 1 tablespoon sugar. Using a serrated knife, cut dough into 8 wedges, but do not separate. Bake 20 to 25 minutes or until a toothpick inserted in center comes out clean. Cool on wire rack. Serve warm or at room temperature. Store in an airtight container.
Yield: 8 scones

DILLY CHEESE SCONES

2 cups all-purpose flour
1 tablespoon baking powder
2 teaspoons dried dill weed
1 teaspoon salt
1/2 teaspoon dry mustard
1/4 cup butter or margarine
1 cup (4 ounces) grated sharp Cheddar cheese
1 cup milk
1 egg
1 teaspoon water

Preheat oven to 425 degrees. In a large bowl, combine first 5 ingredients. Cut in butter with a pastry blender or 2 knives until mixture resembles a coarse meal. Stir in cheese. Make a well in the center of mixture; pour in milk. Mix with a fork just until blended.

With floured hands, turn out dough onto a lightly floured surface and pat out to 1/2-inch thickness. Using a 2-inch round biscuit cutter, cut out scones and place on an ungreased baking sheet. In a small cup, blend egg and water; lightly brush over scones. Bake 12 to 15 minutes or until tops are golden brown. Serve warm.
Yield: about 1 dozen scones
Note: To reheat scones, wrap in aluminum foil and bake 10 minutes at 400 degrees.

CINNAMON-APPLE COFFEE CAKES

 3/4 cup crushed cinnamon graham
     crackers (about five 2 ½ x 5-inch
     crackers)
 3/4 cup chopped walnuts
   2 teaspoons ground cinnamon
   1 package (16 ounces) pound cake
     mix
   1 can (21 ounces) apple pie filling
   2 eggs, beaten
   2 tablespoons sour cream

Preheat oven to 325 degrees. In
a small bowl, mix crushed crackers,
walnuts, and cinnamon. In a large bowl,
combine cake mix, pie filling, eggs, and
sour cream; beat with an electric mixer
until well blended. Spoon 1 tablespoon
graham cracker mixture into bottom of
each greased and floured tin of a 6-mold
fluted tube pan. Spoon 2 rounded
tablespoons batter over cracker mixture.
Spoon 1 tablespoon cracker mixture
over batter. Top with 2 tablespoons
batter. Bake 45 to 50 minutes or until
toothpick inserted into center of cake
comes out clean. Cool in pan 5 minutes;
invert cakes onto a wire rack and
cool completely. Store in an airtight
container.
Yield: twelve 4-inch coffee cakes

BUTTERED ALMOND CAKES

CAKE
 1/2 cup sliced almonds
 1/2 cup butter or margarine, softened
1 1/2 cups granulated sugar, divided
   3 egg yolks
1 1/2 cups all-purpose flour
 1/4 teaspoon baking soda
 1/2 cup sour cream
   1 teaspoon almond extract
   3 egg whites, room temperature

AMARETTO GLAZE
   6 tablespoons butter or margarine
 1/4 cup amaretto
 3/4 cup granulated sugar
   2 tablespoons water

Preheat oven to 325 degrees. Grease
and flour eight 1-cup metal gelatin
molds. Sprinkle almonds in bottoms of
pans.
   In a large bowl, cream butter and
1 1/4 cups sugar. Add egg yolks, one at a
time, beating well after each addition.
In a separate bowl, combine flour and
baking soda. Add to creamed mixture
alternately with sour cream, beginning
and ending with flour mixture. Stir in
almond extract.
   In a medium bowl, beat egg whites
until foamy. Add 1/4 cup sugar, 1
tablespoon at a time, beating until stiff
peaks form. Fold into cake batter. Pour
into pans and bake 20 to 25 minutes,
testing for doneness with a toothpick.
Cool in pans 15 minutes.
   While cakes are cooling in pans,
combine glaze ingredients in a small
saucepan. Boil 4 minutes, stirring
constantly. Remove cakes from pans;
place on a wire rack with waxed paper
spread underneath. While cakes are still
warm, use a fork or wooden skewer to
poke holes in cakes. Spoon warm glaze
over cakes. Allow cakes to sit at least 4
hours or overnight before serving.
   Cake may also be baked in a greased
and floured 9 x 5 x 3-inch loaf pan at
325 degrees for 1 hour and 15 minutes,
testing for doneness with a toothpick.
Yield: about 8 small cakes or 1 loaf

Spicy Apple Cakes are loaded with fresh apple chunks and chopped walnuts.

APPLE CAKES

2 ¼ cups all-purpose flour
¾ teaspoon baking powder
½ teaspoon plus ⅛ teaspoon ground cinnamon, divided
¼ teaspoon salt
¼ teaspoon ground allspice
¼ teaspoon ground nutmeg
¼ cup butter or margarine, softened
¾ cup plus 2 tablespoons granulated sugar, divided
3 eggs
½ cup vegetable oil
1 tablespoon vanilla extract
2 cups peeled, cored, and chopped Granny Smith apples (reserve peel from 1 apple)
½ cup chopped walnuts

Preheat oven to 400 degrees. In a medium bowl, stir together flour, baking powder, ½ teaspoon cinnamon, salt, allspice, and nutmeg. In a large bowl, cream butter and ¾ cup sugar until fluffy. Add eggs, oil, and vanilla; stir until smooth. Add dry ingredients to creamed mixture; stir until well blended. Finely chop reserved apple peel. Stir in apples, apple peel, and walnuts. Spoon batter into paper-lined muffin pan, filling each tin ¾ full. Bake 15 to 18 minutes or until a toothpick inserted in center of cake comes out clean. Transfer to a wire rack. In a small bowl, stir together remaining sugar and cinnamon. Sprinkle tops of warm cakes with sugar mixture. Cool completely. Store in an airtight container.

Yield: about 1½ dozen cakes

Heart shapes add to the sweetness of these Spice Cakes with Honey Icing.

SPICE CAKES WITH HONEY ICING

CAKES
- 1/2 cup butter or margarine, softened
- 1 1/2 cups firmly packed brown sugar
- 3 eggs
- 1 cup sour cream
- 1/2 cup milk
- 2 cups all-purpose flour
- 2 teaspoons ground cinnamon
- 1 1/2 teaspoons baking soda
- 1 teaspoon baking powder
- 1/2 teaspoon ground cloves
- 1/2 teaspoon ground nutmeg
- 1/2 teaspoon salt

ICING
- 1 cup firmly packed brown sugar
- 1 cup butter or margarine
- 1/2 cup honey
- 2 cups sifted confectioners sugar

For cakes, preheat oven to 350 degrees. In a large bowl, cream butter and sugar until fluffy. Add eggs, one at a time, beating well after each addition. Add sour cream and milk; stir until well blended. In a medium bowl, sift together remaining ingredients. Add dry ingredients to creamed mixture, stirring until well blended. Spoon batter into a greased and floured pan containing 3 1/2-inch-wide heart tins. Bake 18 to 20 minutes or until a toothpick inserted in center of cake comes out clean. Cool in pan 10 minutes. Remove cakes from pan. Cool completely on a wire rack.

For icing, combine brown sugar, butter, and honey in a small saucepan. Stirring constantly, cook over medium heat until sugar dissolves. Remove from heat; beat in confectioners sugar. Allow icing to cool 10 minutes. Gently press a 1-inch heart-shaped cookie cutter into center of 1 cake. Icing around cookie cutter, ice top and sides of cake. Remove cookie cutter. Repeat for remaining cakes. Allow icing to cool completely. Store in an airtight container.

Yield: about 1 dozen cakes

29

APPLE-CHEDDAR TURNOVERS

CRUST
1 1/3 cups all-purpose flour
 1/2 teaspoon salt
 1/2 cup butter, chilled and cut into
     pieces
 1/2 cup finely grated mild Cheddar
     cheese
 2 tablespoons ice water

FILLING
 2 apples, peeled, cored, and
     chopped
 6 tablespoons butter or margarine
 1/3 cup firmly packed brown sugar
 1 tablespoon all-purpose flour
 1/2 teaspoon ground cinnamon
 1/4 teaspoon ground cloves
 1 egg yolk
 1 teaspoon water
     Butter or margarine

For crust, sift flour and salt into a mixing bowl. Using a pastry blender or two knives, cut butter into flour until mixture resembles coarse meal. Stir in cheese. Sprinkle ice water over dough, mixing quickly just until dough forms a soft ball. Wrap dough in plastic wrap and refrigerate 1 hour.

For filling, sauté apples in 6 tablespoons butter over medium heat, stirring frequently until apples are soft. Stir in brown sugar, flour, cinnamon, and cloves; stirring constantly, cook 1 minute. Remove from heat and cool completely.

On a lightly floured surface, use a floured rolling pin to roll out dough to 1/8-inch thickness. Cut dough into 4-inch circles (we used the ring from a 4-inch pastry pan with removable bottom). Combine egg yolk and water. Brush pastry circles with egg yolk mixture. Place 1 heaping tablespoon of filling in the center of each circle and dot with butter. Fold pastry over filling, pressing edges to seal. Brush outside of pastry with egg yolk mixture. Cut slits in tops of turnovers for steam to escape. Refrigerate 30 minutes.

Preheat oven to 350 degrees. Bake 20 to 25 minutes or until golden brown.
Yield: about 8 turnovers

HAM AND CHEESE BISCUIT TURNOVERS

⅓ cup diced ham (about 3½ ounces)
⅓ cup shredded Cheddar cheese
2 tablespoons mayonnaise
1 can (7½ ounces) refrigerated buttermilk biscuits (10 count)

Preheat oven to 375 degrees. In a small bowl, combine ham, cheese, and mayonnaise. Press each biscuit into a 3-inch-diameter circle. Spoon about 1 tablespoon ham mixture in center of each biscuit and fold over; press edges together. Place on a greased baking sheet. Use scissors to cut slits in tops of turnovers. Bake 12 to 15 minutes or until golden brown. Serve warm.
Yield: 10 turnovers

QUICHE MUFFINS

1 container (16 ounces) cottage cheese
3 egg whites
5 eggs
¼ cup buttermilk
¼ cup all-purpose flour
1 teaspoon baking powder
¼ teaspoon salt
2 cups (8 ounces) shredded sharp Cheddar cheese
10 slices bacon, cooked and crumbled
2 green onions, chopped

Preheat oven to 400 degrees. Place cottage cheese in a food processor fitted with a steel blade and process until smooth. Transfer to a large bowl. Process egg whites in food processor until foamy. Add next 5 ingredients and process until smooth. Add egg mixture to cottage cheese. Stir in Cheddar cheese, bacon, and onions. Fill greased large muffin tins ⅔ full and bake 12 to 15 minutes or until edges are lightly browned.
Yield: about 10 muffins

MINI CHEDDAR SOUFFLÉS

1 pound white potatoes, peeled and cut into pieces
1/4 cup butter or margarine
1/4 cup all-purpose flour
6 eggs, separated
1/2 teaspoon salt
1/4 teaspoon ground black pepper
1/4 teaspoon cream of tartar
1 3/4 cups (7 ounces) shredded sharp Cheddar cheese

In a large saucepan, cover potatoes with salted water. Bring water to a boil and cook 25 to 30 minutes or until potatoes are tender. Drain, reserving 1 1/2 cups potato water. Process potatoes in a food processor until puréed; leave in processor.

Preheat oven to 375 degrees. In a large saucepan, melt butter over medium heat. Add flour, stirring until smooth. Cook 3 to 4 minutes or until flour begins to brown. Whisk in reserved potato water. Bring to a boil. Stirring occasionally, reduce heat to low and simmer 5 minutes. Add sauce to potato purée and process until well blended. Transfer to a large bowl; whisk in egg yolks, salt, and pepper. In another large bowl, beat egg whites and cream of tartar until stiff peaks form. Fold half of egg white mixture into potato mixture. Fold in cheese and remaining egg white mixture. Spoon into a heavily greased miniature muffin pan, filling each cup three-fourths full. Bake 25 to 30 minutes or until golden brown. Serve warm.
Yield: about 7 dozen mini soufflés

OLIVE-CREAM CHEESE BAGELS

1 cup milk, scalded
1 package (3 ounces) cream cheese, softened
1/4 cup butter or margarine
1 tablespoon sugar
1 teaspoon salt
1 package dry yeast
2 eggs
1/2 cup sliced green olives
4 cups all-purpose flour
Cream cheese to serve

In a medium saucepan, combine milk, cream cheese, butter, sugar, and salt. Cook over medium-low heat, stirring occasionally, until mixture reaches 115 degrees. Remove from heat; transfer to a large bowl. Add yeast and stir until dissolved. Let stand 3 minutes. Whisk eggs into milk mixture. Stir in olives. Gradually stir in flour. Turn onto a lightly floured surface and knead 5 to 10 minutes or until dough becomes smooth and elastic. Shape into a ball and place in a greased bowl. Grease top of dough, cover, and let rise in a warm place (80 to 85 degrees) 30 minutes.

Turn dough onto a lightly floured surface and punch down. For each bagel, pinch off about 2 tablespoons dough and shape into a 5-inch-long roll. Form dough into a ring, overlap ends, and pinch ends to seal. (Or, using a floured rolling pin, roll out dough to 1/2-inch thickness. Use a 2-inch biscuit cutter to cut out dough. Use the end of a

(Continued on page 33.)

Green olives lend distinctive flavor to Olive-Cream Cheese Bagels.

(Continued from page 32.) wooden spoon to punch a hole through center of each bagel.) Place on a greased baking sheet. Cover and let rise in a warm place 10 minutes or until puffy.

Preheat oven to 400 degrees. Fill a large saucepan with water; bring to a boil. Drop 4 to 5 bagels at a time into boiling water and cook 3 minutes, turning once. Transfer to a greased baking sheet. Bake 25 to 30 minutes or until golden brown. Serve warm or at room temperature with cream cheese. **Yield:** about 2$^1/_2$ dozen bagels

BUTTERSCOTCH COFFEE CAKE

- 1   package (25 ounces) frozen white dinner rolls
- 1/2   cup sugar
- 1   package (3.5 ounces) butterscotch pudding and pie filling mix
- 1   tablespoon ground cinnamon
- 1/2   cup butter or margarine, melted
- 1   cup chopped pecans

Place frozen rolls in bottom of a greased 12-cup fluted tube pan. In a small bowl, combine sugar, pudding mix, and cinnamon. Sprinkle sugar mixture over rolls. Pour butter over sugar mixture. Sprinkle pecans on top. Cover with plastic wrap and let rise in a warm place (80 to 85 degrees) 5 1/2 to 6 1/2 hours or until doubled in size. To serve in early morning, coffee cake can rise overnight (about 8 hours).

Preheat oven to 350 degrees. Bake 30 to 35 minutes or until golden brown. Remove from oven and immediately invert onto plate. Serve warm.

Yield: about 16 servings

SPICY CARROT CUPCAKES

- 1   package (18.25 ounces) spice cake mix
- 1 1/3   cups water
- 3   eggs
- 1/3   cup vegetable oil
- 1 3/4   cups finely shredded carrots (about 4 carrots)
- 3/4   cup finely chopped toasted walnuts, divided
- 1   cup flaked coconut, toasted and divided
- 2   packages (3 ounces each) cream cheese, softened
- 1/3   cup butter or margarine, softened
- 3   tablespoons sifted confectioners sugar
- 1 1/2   tablespoons maple syrup

Preheat oven to 350 degrees. In a large bowl, combine cake mix, water, eggs, and oil. Beat at low speed of an electric mixer 30 seconds. Beat at medium speed 2 minutes. Stir in carrots, 1/2 cup walnuts, and 1/2 cup coconut. Fill paper-lined muffin cups about three-fourths full. Bake 15 to 20 minutes or until a toothpick inserted in center of cupcake comes out clean. Transfer cupcakes to a wire rack to cool.

In a small bowl, beat cream cheese and butter until fluffy. Add confectioners sugar and maple syrup; continue to beat until smooth. Ice cupcakes. Sprinkle remaining 1/4 cup walnuts and 1/2 cup coconut over icing. Store in an airtight container in refrigerator.

Yield: about 2 1/2 dozen cupcakes

CINNAMON-SUGAR PRETZELS

2 loaves (one 32-ounce package) frozen white bread dough, thawed according to package directions
  Vegetable cooking spray
1 cup granulated sugar
1 teaspoon ground cinnamon

On a lightly floured surface, use a floured rolling pin to roll out each loaf to a 6 x 12-inch rectangle. Cut dough into twenty-four 1 x 6-inch strips. Shape each strip into a 14-inch-long roll. Refer to Fig. 1 and shape each roll into a pretzel shape.

Fig. 1

Place pretzels 1 inch apart on a baking sheet sprayed with cooking spray. Spray tops of pretzels with cooking spray, cover, and let rise in a warm place (80 to 85 degrees) 1 hour or until doubled in size.

In a medium bowl, combine sugar and cinnamon; set aside.

Preheat oven to 350 degrees. Bake 18 to 20 minutes or until golden brown. Lightly spray both sides of pretzels with cooking spray. Place pretzels, one at a time, in sugar mixture and spoon sugar over until well coated. Transfer to a wire rack to cool completely. Store in an airtight container.
Yield: 2 dozen pretzels

SOFT PRETZELS

$1^1/_2$ cups warm water
1 package dry yeast
1 tablespoon granulated sugar
$4^1/_2$ cups all-purpose flour
$1^1/_2$ teaspoons salt
1 egg, lightly beaten
  Coarsely ground kosher or sea salt

Combine water, yeast, and sugar in a mixing bowl. Allow to stand until yeast is dissolved and begins to foam (about 5 minutes). Stir in flour and $1^1/_2$ teaspoons salt. Turn out onto lightly floured surface and knead 8 to 10 minutes or until dough is smooth and elastic. Separate dough into 16 equal pieces. Roll each piece into a 20-inch-long rope and form into a pretzel shape. Place on a lightly greased baking sheet. Cover and let rise 20 minutes.

Preheat oven to 425 degrees. Brush pretzels with egg and sprinkle with coarsely ground salt. Bake 15 minutes or until golden brown. Remove pretzels from baking sheet and cool on wire rack.
Yield: 16 pretzels

HONEY-CHEESE ROLLS

- 8 cups all-purpose flour, divided
- 2 teaspoons salt
- 2 packages dry yeast
- 3/4 cup butter or margarine, divided
- 2 cups (8 ounces) shredded Cheddar cheese
- 1 1/2 cups milk
- 1/3 cup honey
- 3 eggs

In a large bowl, combine 6 cups flour, salt, and yeast; stir until well blended. In a medium saucepan, combine 1/2 cup butter, cheese, milk, and honey. Cook over medium heat until a thermometer registers 130 degrees (butter may not be completely melted). Add eggs and cheese mixture alternately to dry ingredients, stirring until a soft dough forms. Gradually stir in remaining flour. Turn dough onto a lightly floured surface; knead about 10 minutes or until dough becomes soft and elastic. Transfer to a large greased bowl. Melt remaining butter in a small saucepan over low heat. Brush top of dough with 1/2 of melted butter and cover. Let rise in a warm place (80 to 85 degrees) 1 hour or until doubled in size.

Turn dough onto a lightly floured surface and punch down. Shape dough into 3-inch balls and place with sides touching in greased 9-inch round cake pans. If necessary, remelt remaining butter. Brush tops of rolls with melted butter and cover. Let rise about 1 hour or until doubled in size.

Preheat oven to 375 degrees. Bake 30 to 35 minutes or until golden brown. Cool completely in pan. Store in an airtight container.

Yield: about 2 dozen rolls
To serve: Preheat oven to 350 degrees. Bake rolls, uncovered, 3 to 5 minutes or until heated through.

BRIOCHE ROLLS

- 2 packages dry yeast
- 1/4 cup warm water
- 1/2 cup butter or margarine, softened
- 1/3 cup granulated sugar
- 1/2 teaspoon salt
- 1/2 cup evaporated milk
- 3 1/2 cups all-purpose flour, divided
- 4 eggs
- 1 tablespoon granulated sugar

Dissolve yeast in warm water. In a medium mixing bowl, cream butter, 1/3 cup sugar, and salt until fluffy. Stir in milk and 1 cup flour. In another medium bowl, beat 3 eggs and 1 egg yolk (reserve egg white). Add yeast and eggs to creamed mixture, beating until well blended. Stir in remaining 2 1/2 cups flour. Turn out dough onto a lightly floured surface and knead 3 to 5 minutes or until dough holds together. Place in lightly greased bowl, turning to coat entire surface. Cover and let rise in a warm place 1 hour or until doubled in size.

Punch down dough. Divide dough into fourths. Reserving one fourth, pull remaining dough into 24 equal pieces. Roll pieces into balls and place in greased muffin pans or fluted tart pans. Pull reserved dough into 24 pieces and roll pieces into small balls. Make indentation with thumb in top of each larger roll and press smaller ball into each indentation. Cover and let rise 45 minutes or until doubled in size.

Preheat oven to 375 degrees. Lightly beat reserved egg white with 1 tablespoon sugar; brush on tops of rolls. Bake 20 to 25 minutes or until golden brown.

Yield: 2 dozen rolls

Rich, buttery Brioche Rolls get their beautiful shape from placing a tiny ball of dough into an indentation on each roll before baking.

MUSTARD ROLLS

    2 packages dry yeast
  $1/4$ cup warm water
    1 tablespoon sugar
    1 cup milk
  $2/3$ cup prepared mustard
    2 tablespoons butter or margarine
    4 cups all-purpose flour
       Vegetable cooking spray
    1 egg yolk
    1 tablespoon water

In a small bowl, combine yeast, $1/4$ cup warm water, and sugar; stir until well blended. In a small saucepan, heat milk, mustard, and butter over medium-high heat until butter melts. In a large bowl, combine yeast mixture, milk mixture, and flour. Stir until a soft dough forms. Turn onto a lightly floured surface and knead about 8 minutes or until dough becomes smooth and elastic. Place in a large bowl sprayed with cooking spray, turning once to coat top of dough. Cover and let rise in a warm place (80 to 85 degrees) 1 hour or until doubled in size.

Turn dough onto a lightly floured surface and punch down. Shape dough into $1^1/2$-inch balls and place 2 inches apart on a greased baking sheet. Lightly spray tops of rolls with cooking spray. Cover and let rise in a warm place 1 hour or until doubled in size.

Preheat oven to 400 degrees. In a small bowl, whisk egg yolk with 1 tablespoon water; brush over tops of rolls. Bake 12 to 15 minutes or until golden brown. Serve warm.
Yield: about $3^1/2$ dozen rolls

REFRIGERATOR ROLLS

    1 package active dry yeast
    2 cups warm water
  $3/4$ cup butter or margarine, melted
       and slightly cooled
  $1/4$ cup granulated sugar
    1 egg, beaten
    4 cups self-rising flour

In a small bowl, dissolve yeast in warm water. In a large bowl, blend butter with sugar. Stir in yeast mixture and egg. Add flour, stirring just until blended. Store covered in refrigerator at least 2 hours before using or up to 5 days.
Yield: batter for $1^1/2$ dozen rolls
To bake rolls: Fill greased muffin pan two-thirds full with batter. Cover with a towel and let sit 30 minutes. Bake 20 to 25 minutes at 350 degrees or until lightly browned. If desired, brush with melted butter before serving.

OATMEAL-RYE ROLLS

2 cups water
1 cup old-fashioned rolled oats
3 cups all-purpose flour
2 cups whole-wheat flour
1 cup rye flour
$1/2$ cup nonfat dry milk
$2^1/2$ teaspoons salt
2 packages rapid-rising dry yeast
$1/3$ cup warm water
$1/2$ cup honey
$1/4$ cup vegetable oil
   Vegetable cooking spray

In a medium saucepan, bring 2 cups water to a boil over high heat. Remove from heat; stir in oats. Cool to room temperature.

In a large bowl, sift together flours, dry milk, and salt. In a small bowl, dissolve yeast in $1/3$ cup warm water. Add oats mixture, yeast mixture, honey, and oil to dry ingredients. Stir until a soft dough forms. Turn onto a lightly floured surface and knead until dough becomes smooth and elastic. Place in a large bowl sprayed with cooking spray, turning once to coat top of dough. Cover and let rise in a warm place (80 to 85 degrees) 1 hour or until doubled in size. Turn dough onto a lightly floured surface and punch down. Shape dough into 2-inch balls and place 2 inches apart on a greased baking sheet. Spray tops of rolls with cooking spray, cover, and let rise in a warm place 1 hour or until doubled in size.

Preheat oven to 350 degrees. Bake 25 to 30 minutes or until golden brown. Serve warm or cool completely on a wire rack.

Yield: about 2 dozen rolls

HOT GARLIC-CHEESE LOAVES

$3^1/2$ cups buttermilk baking mix
$2^1/2$ cups (10 ounces) shredded sharp Cheddar cheese
1 teaspoon garlic powder
$1/4$ teaspoon ground red pepper
$1^1/4$ cups milk
2 eggs, beaten

Preheat oven to 350 degrees. In a large bowl, combine baking mix, cheese, garlic powder, and red pepper. Add milk and eggs to dry ingredients; mix only until ingredients are moistened. Spoon batter into 4 greased and floured $3^1/4$ x 6-inch baking pans. Bake 30 to 35 minutes or until lightly browned. Cool in pans 5 minutes. Remove from pans and cool completely on a wire rack. Store in an airtight container.

Yield: 4 mini loaves bread

CORNMEAL YEAST MUFFINS

1 package dry yeast
1/4 cup plus 1 teaspoon sugar, divided
1/3 cup warm water (105 to 115 degrees)
1 cup milk
1/2 cup butter or margarine
1 1/2 teaspoons salt
1 can (15 1/4 ounces) whole kernel corn, drained
1 cup cream-style corn
2 eggs, beaten
1 1/2 cups yellow cornmeal
3 cups all-purpose flour

In a small bowl, dissolve yeast and 1 teaspoon sugar in warm water. In a small saucepan, combine milk, butter, remaining 1/4 cup sugar, and salt over medium heat; whisk until butter melts and sugar is dissolved. Remove from heat and pour into a large bowl. Add whole kernel corn, cream-style corn, eggs, and yeast mixture; stir until well blended. Add cornmeal and flour, 1 cup at a time; stir until a thick batter forms. Cover and let rise in a warm place (80 to 85 degrees) 1 to 1 1/2 hours or until almost doubled in size.

Stir batter down. Spoon batter into greased muffin cups, filling each two-thirds full. Let rise uncovered in a warm place about 45 minutes.

Preheat oven to 375 degrees. Bake 20 to 25 minutes or until golden brown. Allow muffins to cool in pan 5 minutes. Serve warm or transfer to a wire rack to cool completely.
Yield: about 2 dozen muffins

SPICY CORN WAFERS

1 1/2 cups white cornmeal
1 teaspoon garlic powder
3/4 teaspoon salt
1/2 teaspoon ground red pepper
2 1/4 cups boiling water
4 tablespoons butter or margarine, melted

Preheat oven to 425 degrees. In a medium bowl, combine cornmeal, garlic powder, salt, and red pepper. Stirring constantly, pour boiling water over dry ingredients and mix well; stir in melted butter. For each wafer, drop 1 tablespoon batter onto an ungreased nonstick baking sheet. Using back of spoon, spread batter to form a 3-inch circle; add hot water to thin batter if necessary. Bake 18 to 20 minutes or until edges are golden brown. Serve warm.
Yield: about 3 dozen wafers

ANGEL BISCUITS

2 1/2 cups biscuit baking mix
 1/2 cup sweetened shredded coconut
1 cup whipping cream
2 tablespoons butter or margarine, melted

Preheat oven to 450 degrees. In a large bowl, combine baking mix and coconut. Add cream and stir until well blended. Turn dough onto a lightly floured surface and knead about 1 minute. Use a floured rolling pin to roll out dough to 1/2-inch thickness. Use a floured 2-inch biscuit cutter to cut out dough. Place biscuits 2 inches apart on a greased baking sheet and brush tops with melted butter. Bake 7 to 10 minutes or until light brown. Transfer to a wire rack to cool completely. Store in an airtight container.

To serve, preheat oven to 350 degrees. Cover and bake 3 to 5 minutes or until heated through.

Yield: about 1 1/2 dozen biscuits

HOMESTYLE SWEET POTATO BISCUITS

2 cups all-purpose flour
2 1/2 teaspoons baking powder
 1/2 teaspoon salt
 1/4 cup chilled butter or margarine
 1/4 cup vegetable shortening
1 cup cooked, mashed sweet potatoes
5 to 7 tablespoons buttermilk

Preheat oven to 450 degrees. In a large bowl, combine flour, baking powder, and salt. Using a pastry blender or 2 knives, cut in butter and shortening until well blended. Add sweet potatoes and enough buttermilk to make a soft dough. Lightly knead dough about 20 times. On a lightly floured surface, roll out dough to 1/2-inch thickness. Use a 2-inch biscuit cutter to cut out biscuits. Bake on an ungreased baking sheet 12 to 15 minutes or until biscuits are light golden brown. Serve warm.

Yield: about 2 dozen biscuits

Little Orange Slice Cakes are packed with the goodness of gumdrop candies, walnuts, dates, and flaked coconut.

ORANGE SLICE CAKES

1 package (18 ounces) orange slice gumdrop candies
2 cups chopped walnuts
1 package (8 ounces) chopped dates
1 can (3^1/$_2$ ounces) flaked coconut
3^1/$_4$ cups all-purpose flour, divided
1 teaspoon baking soda
^{1}/$_2$ teaspoon salt
1 cup butter or margarine, softened
1^1/$_2$ cups granulated sugar
^{1}/$_2$ cup firmly packed brown sugar
4 eggs
1 teaspoon vanilla extract
1 cup buttermilk
^{3}/$_4$ cup sifted confectioners sugar
^{1}/$_3$ cup orange juice
1 teaspoon grated orange zest

Preheat oven to 300 degrees. Line 2^1/$_2$ x 4-inch loaf pans with aluminum foil loaf baking cups. Reserve 7 candies; chop remaining candies. On a sugared surface, use a rolling pin to roll out reserved candies to ^{1}/$_8$-inch thickness. Cut out "petals" using a teardrop-shaped aspic cutter; set aside.

In a medium bowl, combine chopped candies, walnuts, dates, and coconut. Add ^{1}/$_2$ cup flour; stir until mixture is coated. In another medium bowl, combine remaining 2^3/$_4$ cups flour, baking soda, and salt. In a large bowl, cream butter, granulated sugar, and brown sugar until fluffy. Add eggs and vanilla; beat until smooth. Alternately beat dry ingredients and buttermilk into creamed mixture, beating until well blended. Stir in fruit and nut mixture. Spoon batter into prepared pans. Place 5 candy petals on each cake. Bake 45 to 55 minutes or until a toothpick inserted in center of cake comes out clean.

In a small bowl, combine confectioners sugar, orange juice, and orange zest; whisk until smooth. Use a wooden skewer to poke holes about 1 inch apart in top of each warm cake. Spoon about 1 teaspoon glaze over each cake. Store in an airtight container.
Yield: about 18 small cakes

Orange-Pecan Pumpkin Bars are a great alternative to pumpkin pie.

ORANGE-PECAN PUMPKIN BARS

1 package (18.25 ounces) yellow cake mix
1/4 cup butter or margarine, melted
1/2 cup finely chopped pecans
3/4 cup orange marmalade, melted
2 packages (3 ounces each) cream cheese, softened
1 cup canned pumpkin
1/4 cup firmly packed brown sugar
1 egg
1 teaspoon vanilla extract
1/8 teaspoon salt

Preheat oven to 350 degrees. In a medium bowl, combine cake mix and melted butter (mixture will be crumbly). Stir in pecans. Reserve 1 cup cake mix mixture for topping. Press remaining mixture into bottom of a greased 9 x 13-inch baking pan. Spread marmalade over crust. In a medium bowl, beat cream cheese until fluffy. Add remaining ingredients; beat until smooth. Spread filling over marmalade layer. Sprinkle reserved cake mix mixture over filling. Bake 40 to 45 minutes or until top is lightly browned and filling is set. Cool in pan on a wire rack. Cut into 1 x 2-inch bars. Store in an airtight container in refrigerator.

Yield: about 4 dozen bars

MARASCHINO CHERRY BREAD

- 1 jar (10 ounces) maraschino cherries
- 1 cup granulated sugar
- 2 eggs
- $^1/_4$ cup vegetable oil
- 1 teaspoon vanilla extract
- $1^3/_4$ cups all-purpose flour
- $1^1/_2$ teaspoons baking powder
- $^1/_4$ teaspoon salt
- 1 cup chopped pecans
- 1 cup sifted confectioners sugar

Preheat oven to 350 degrees. Grease two $3^1/_2$ x $7^1/_2$-inch loaf pans and line with waxed paper. Drain cherries, reserving juice. Chop cherries; reserve 1 tablespoon for glaze. In a large bowl, combine granulated sugar, eggs, oil, vanilla, chopped cherries, and $^1/_4$ cup reserved cherry juice; beat until well blended. In a small bowl, combine flour, baking powder, and salt. Add dry ingredients to cherry mixture; stir until well blended. Stir in pecans. Spoon batter into prepared pans. Bake 45 to 50 minutes or until a toothpick inserted in center of bread comes out clean and top is golden brown. Cool in pans 10 minutes. Remove from pans and place on a wire rack with waxed paper underneath to cool completely.

Combine confectioners sugar, 2 to $2^1/_2$ tablespoons reserved cherry juice, and reserved chopped cherries in a small bowl; stir until well blended. Spoon over bread. Allow icing to harden. Store in an airtight container.

Yield: 2 loaves bread

FUDGY CHOCOLATE CHIP CUPCAKES

CUPCAKES
- $^3/_4$ cup butter or margarine, softened
- $^1/_2$ cup sugar
- 3 eggs
- 1 teaspoon vanilla extract
- $^3/_4$ cup plus 2 tablespoons all-purpose flour
- $^1/_2$ teaspoon baking soda
- $^1/_4$ teaspoon salt
- $^3/_4$ cup buttermilk
- 12 ounces semisweet baking chocolate, melted
- 1 package (12 ounces) semisweet chocolate mini chips

ICING
- 2 cups sugar
- $^1/_4$ cup cocoa
- $^1/_2$ cup butter or margarine
- $^1/_2$ cup milk
- 1 tablespoon light corn syrup
- 1 teaspoon vanilla extract

Preheat oven to 350 degrees. For cupcakes, cream butter and sugar in a large bowl until fluffy. Add eggs and vanilla; beat until well blended. In a small bowl, combine flour, baking soda, and salt. Alternately add dry ingredients, buttermilk, and melted chocolate to creamed mixture; beat until well blended. Stir in chocolate chips. Spoon batter into paper-lined muffin cups. Bake 18 to 22 minutes or until a toothpick inserted near center of cupcake comes out with a few crumbs clinging to it. Cool in pan 10 minutes; transfer cupcakes to a wire rack to cool completely.

For icing, combine sugar and cocoa in a medium saucepan. Add butter, milk, and corn syrup. Stirring constantly, bring to a boil over medium heat; boil 2 minutes. Transfer icing to a medium heat-resistant bowl; cool 5 minutes. Add vanilla. Place icing over a bowl of ice and beat with electric mixer about 5 minutes or until icing is thick enough to spread. Ice cupcakes, using about 1 tablespoon icing for each cupcake. Allow icing to harden. Store in an airtight container in a cool place.

Yield: about 2 dozen cupcakes

SNOWBALL CUPCAKES

  1 package (18.25 ounces) yellow cake mix
  3 eggs
$^1/_3$ cup vegetable oil
  1 can (8 ½ ounces) cream of coconut
  1 cup sour cream
  1 package (7.2 ounces) fluffy white frosting mix
$1^3/_4$ cups flaked coconut
    Candied cherry halves to decorate

Preheat oven to 350 degrees. Combine cake mix, eggs, and oil in a large bowl; beat until well blended. Add cream of coconut and sour cream; beat until smooth. Line muffin pan with aluminum foil muffin cups; fill cups half full. Bake 16 to 18 minutes or until a toothpick inserted in center of cupcake comes out clean. Cool in pan on a wire rack.

In a medium bowl, prepare frosting according to package directions. Dip tops of cupcakes into icing, then into coconut. Decorate with candied cherry halves. Store in a single layer in an airtight container.

Yield: about 3 dozen cupcakes

ORANGE SURPRISE CUPCAKES

These moist cupcakes have a secret hidden in the middle—a filling of cream cheese and chocolate chips.

  2 packages (3 ounces each) cream cheese, softened
$^1/_4$ cup sugar
  1 egg white
$^2/_3$ cup semisweet chocolate mini chips
  1 package (18.25 ounces) orange cake mix
$1^1/_3$ cups water
  3 eggs
$^1/_3$ cup vegetable oil

Preheat oven to 350 degrees. In a medium bowl, beat cream cheese, sugar, and egg white until fluffy. Stir in chocolate chips. In a large bowl, combine cake mix, water, eggs, and oil. Beat at low speed of an electric mixer 30 seconds. Beat at medium speed 2 minutes. Spoon batter into paper-lined muffin cups, filling each about two-thirds full. Drop a tablespoonful of cream cheese mixture into center of batter in each muffin cup. Bake 18 to 21 minutes or until cake springs back when lightly touched. Transfer cupcakes to a wire rack to cool. Store in an airtight container in refrigerator.

Yield: about 2 dozen cupcakes

SANTA CUPCAKES

CUPCAKES
- ¹/₂ cup butter or margarine, softened
- ³/₄ cup firmly packed brown sugar
- 2 eggs
- 1 teaspoon vanilla extract
- 1 cup milk
- ¹/₂ cup frozen apple juice concentrate, thawed
- 2¹/₄ cups all-purpose flour
- ¹/₂ cup cocoa
- ³/₄ teaspoon baking soda
- ¹/₂ teaspoon salt

FROSTING
- ³/₄ cup butter or margarine, softened
- 6³/₄ cups confectioners sugar
- ¹/₂ cup milk
- 1 teaspoon vanilla extract
- Candied cherries, halved
- Raisins
- Red paste food coloring

Scrumptious chocolate Santa Cupcakes are adorned with icing, candied cherries, and raisins to resemble the jolly old gent's cheerful face.

For cupcakes, preheat oven to 375 degrees. In a large bowl, cream butter and brown sugar until fluffy. Add eggs and vanilla; stir until smooth. Stir in milk and apple juice. In a medium bowl, combine flour, cocoa, baking soda, and salt. Add dry ingredients to creamed mixture; stir until well blended. Spoon batter into a paper-lined muffin pan, filling each cup three-fourths full. Bake 18 to 20 minutes or until a toothpick inserted in center of cake comes out clean. Transfer to a wire rack to cool completely.

For frosting, combine butter, confectioners sugar, milk, and vanilla; stir until smooth. Spread a thin layer of frosting over tops of cupcakes. Press cherries and raisins onto frosting for noses and eyes. Transfer 1 cup remaining frosting to a small bowl; tint red. Spoon red and remaining white frosting into separate pastry bags fitted with large star tips. Pipe red frosting onto cupcakes for caps. Pipe white frosting onto cupcakes for trim and beards. Store in an airtight container.

Yield: about 1¹/₂ dozen cupcakes

METRIC EQUIVALENTS

The recipes that appear in this cookbook use the standard United States method for measuring liquid and dry or solid ingredients (teaspoons, tablespoons, and cups). The information on this chart is provided to help cooks outside the U.S. successfully use these recipes. All equivalents are approximate.

METRIC EQUIVALENTS FOR DIFFERENT TYPES OF INGREDIENTS

A standard cup measure of a dry or solid ingredient will vary in weight depending on the type of ingredient. A standard cup of liquid is the same volume for any type of liquid. Use the following chart when converting standard cup measures to grams (weight) or milliliters (volume).

Standard Cup	Fine Powder	Grain	Granular	Liquid Solids	Liquid
	(ex. flour)	(ex. rice)	(ex. sugar)	(ex. butter)	(ex. milk)
1	140 g	150 g	190 g	200 g	240 ml
¾	105 g	113 g	143 g	150 g	180 ml
⅔	93 g	100 g	125 g	133 g	160 ml
½	70 g	75 g	95 g	100 g	120 ml
⅓	47 g	50 g	63 g	67 g	80 ml
¼	35 g	38 g	48 g	50 g	60 ml
⅛	18 g	19 g	24 g	25 g	30 ml

USEFUL EQUIVALENTS FOR LIQUID INGREDIENTS BY VOLUME

¼ tsp				=	1 ml			
½ tsp				=	2 ml			
1 tsp				=	5 ml			
3 tsp	=	1 tbls		=	½ fl oz	=	15 ml	
		2 tbls	=	⅛ cup	=	1 fl oz	=	30 ml
		4 tbls	=	¼ cup	=	2 fl oz	=	60 ml
		5⅓ tbls	=	⅓ cup	=	3 fl oz	=	80 ml
		8 tbls	=	½ cup	=	4 fl oz	=	120 ml
		10⅔ tbls	=	⅔ cup	=	5 fl oz	=	160 ml
		12 tbls	=	¾ cup	=	6 fl oz	=	180 ml
		16 tbls	=	1 cup	=	8 fl oz	=	240 ml
	1 pt	=	2 cups	=	16 fl oz	=	480 ml	
	1 qt	=	4 cups	=	32 fl oz	=	960 ml	
					33 fl oz	=	1000 ml	= 1 l

USEFUL EQUIVALENTS FOR DRY INGREDIENTS BY WEIGHT

(To convert ounces to grams, multiply the number of ounces by 30.)

1 oz	=	¹⁄₁₆ lb	=	30 g
4 oz	=	¼ lb	=	120 g
8 oz	=	½ lb	=	240 g
12 oz	=	¾ lb	=	360 g
16 oz	=	1 lb	=	480 g

USEFUL EQUIVALENTS FOR LENGTH

(To convert inches to centimeters, multiply the number of inches by 2.5.)

1 in				=	2.5 cm	
6 in	=	½ ft		=	15 cm	
12 in	=	1 ft		=	30 cm	
36 in	=	3 ft	= 1 yd	=	90 cm	
40 in				=	100 cm	= 1 m

USEFUL EQUIVALENTS FOR COOKING/OVEN TEMPERATURES

	Fahrenheit	Celsius	Gas Mark
Freeze Water	32° F	0° C	
Room Temperature	68° F	20° C	
Boil Water	212° F	100° C	
Bake	325° F	160° C	3
	350° F	180° C	4
	375° F	190° C	5
	400° F	200° C	6
	425° F	220° C	7
	450° F	230° C	8
Broil			Grill

CUPCAKES & MORE • RECIPE INDEX